The Fourth Nephite Effect

By

Jeffrey Erickson

Dedication

To my wife Christine—You are truly one of the
greatest Fourth Nephites I have ever known.

.

Contents

Title Page -

Acknowledgments

I am grateful for the "greater views" of the Book of Mormon. These views, insights, principles and doctrines of Christ have taught me how to live more purposefully and powerfully.

The Lord has blessed me with numerous fourth Nephites in my life. I am grateful to every one of those people who have inspired me, supported me, and shaped my life through their example. I have felt the goodness of God through their prayers, thoughts, actions, and lives time and time again.

I am thankful for people who have worked hard to cultivate and develop skills that are life changing.

Holly Banks is one of these people, as she continues to edit, revise, alter, and adjust the ideas and words to make the text more powerful and enlightening. Marjorie Harris is another one of these skilled people, who always powerfully edits and never complains. These two individuals are encouraging and always inspire me to write more powerfully and with more purpose.

May this book enable you to see the fourth Nephites in your life, and at times, be one.

~Jeff

Prologue:

Shortly after completing this book, my ward at church held our annual primary program. All the children sang beautiful musical numbers and many extended family members were there in attendance to support them. When the sacrament service ended, I saw the grandmother of some of the participating children in the congregation. This was not just any grandmother, though; this was Dinah—one of the most influential people in my young life.

When I was a teenager, Dinah and her family moved into my ward. Her husband was my teacher's quorum advisor, and she and her family welcomed me in as a dear family friend. They invited me to family functions, took me on family trips, and nearly adopted me as one of their own. They were a blessing and example to me during a time when I was struggling through my parents' divorce, and my mother was going to school and working full-time.

I seem to bump into this wonderful woman every few years. But for me, this particular occasion was different; I had recently finished writing this book and had been reflecting on those who rescue and save those around them. I was so thrilled to see one of my own lifesavers, if you will. Memories of what she and her family had done for me flooded my mind. I was filled with the spirit of gratitude for her efforts and sacrifices on my behalf. We spoke for a few minutes in the chapel and got caught up, and then suddenly I got very serious.

I said, "Dinah, I need to tell you something that I should have told you before". I looked her in the eyes and said, "I know I have never told you this, but I want you to know that you saved me". The spirit filled my heart and I told her I loved her, and then I got too emotional to speak. It was a very tender moment. I was extremely grateful to have the chance to express gratitude to Dinah for helping me when I needed it most. I am indebted to my Heavenly Father for allowing me to have this treasured experience on a sacred Sunday afternoon.

I am forever grateful for the Dinah's in our lives. Dinah will always be one of the "Fourth

Nephites" of my life. These emissaries of Christ are sent to minister to us when the Savior knows we need it the most, and they are who this book is about. May we learn to recognize them, know them, and be them.

The Fourth Nephite Effect

As a full-time missionary, my companion and I were traveling home in our car one night in a rural area of Sydney, Nova Scotia. It was dark, snow was falling, and the roads became very slick. Being from Arizona, driving in snow was a challenge for me; suddenly, I lost control of the car, and we went off the road into a ditch on the right side of the road. Gratefully, both the car and my companion and I were unharmed, but we quickly realized we were in a tough spot. It was late at night on a very cold evening. These were not the days of cell phones and OnStar emergency systems when we were one call away from help.

It was late enough that minimal traffic was coming or going on this rural highway. My companion and I climbed out of the car and scrambled up to the road wondering what to do.

I don't remember all of the details or what we immediately did, and I don't even remember having much time to pray, but I am certain I uttered a quick, silent prayer.

I remember making the climb up to the road, and—in that very instant—a truck slowed down and pulled up to us on the side of the road. The driver got out of the truck, assessed the situation, said a few words, and jumped back in his truck. It turned out the driver was driving a tow truck. He pulled forward on the road in front of our car and proceeded to release his tow chain and tow bar, walk it down to the front of our little car, and hook it up. He then pulled our car from the ditch and back up onto the road.

Before we could even say anything, he jumped out of his truck, unhooked our car, and started walking back to his truck. We ran to thank him and offered to pay him, but he refused and jumped in his truck and departed as quickly as he came. Just like that, we were back on our way. What could have been a serious emergency was solved in a matter of minutes!

This man performed a remarkable service for us on a dark, cold night in a desperate time of need. I don't think we realized how bad of a spot we were in, but Heavenly Father did, and He sent someone—almost like *a fourth Nephite*—to arrive and deliver us from our difficult predicament. Let me explain what I mean.

In the 28ᵗʰ chapter of Third Nephi, Mormon tells us the story of the three Nephites. These three anonymous Nephites were devoted followers and faithful servants of Christ for many years. When Christ came to the temple among the Nephites after His resurrection, these three were called among His twelve disciples. When it was time for the Savior to return to His Father, He turned to these three disciples and asked, "What will ye that I should do unto you, when I am gone unto the Father?" (3 Nephi 28:4). The scriptures say, "And they sorrowed in their hearts, for they durst not speak unto him the thing which they desired" (3 Nephi 28:5). The Savior then answered His own question by reading their thoughts, "And he said unto them: Behold, I know your thoughts, and ye have desired the thing which John, my beloved, who was with me in my ministry, before that I was lifted up by the Jews, desired of me" (3 Nephi 28:6).

What were those thoughts and desires that these Nephites shared with John? The Savior explained, "And again, ye shall not have pain while ye shall dwell in the flesh, neither sorrow save it be for the sins of the world; and all this will I do because of the thing which ye have desired of me, for ye have desired that ye might bring the souls of men unto me, while the world shall stand" (3 Nephi 28:9). These three Nephites loved their callings, responsibilities, and their spiritual labors so deeply that they never wanted them to end. They wanted to serve as long as "the world shall stand." They wanted their fellow saints and every soul to come unto Christ.

The scriptures then tell us, "they did again minister upon the face of the earth... they did go forth upon the face of the land, and did minister unto all the people, uniting as many to the church as would believe in their preaching; baptizing them, and as many as were baptized did receive the Holy Ghost" (3 Nephi 28:16,18). Since the time of the Savior's sacred promise to them, they have been serving, succoring, testifying, rescuing, comforting, delivering and inviting all to come unto Christ.

Here is one modern example of their ministering efforts:

Shortly after beginning to assist Joseph Smith with the work of translation, Oliver wrote to David Whitmer in Fayette township.

He enthusiastically testified that Joseph Smith had the ancient records and that the work was divine. Soon he sent a few lines of the translation and bore witness that he knew the plates contained a record of the people who once inhabited this continent.

David Whitmer, then twenty-four years of age, eagerly showed these letters to his parents and brothers and sisters. Persecution began to intensify in the Harmony area, so late in May, Oliver communicated with David about the possibility of Joseph and Oliver going to stay with the Whitmers in Fayette.

In response Peter Whitmer, Sr., David's father, invited Joseph to stay at his farm home as long as was needed to finish the work of translation. David's brother John offered to help as Joseph's scribe. Many people in the Fayette area were anxious to hear more about the work.

A late May planting was essential for successful fall crops; therefore, David Whitmer had to plow and prepare the soil before he could take his two-horse wagon to pick up Joseph Smith and Oliver Cowdery. At the end of a day of plowing he found he had accomplished in one day what normally would have taken two days to do. David's father was likewise impressed by this apparent miracle. Peter Whitmer, Sr., said, 'There must be an overruling hand in this, and I think you would better go down to Pennsylvania as soon as your plaster of paris is sown (Plaster of paris was used to reduce the acidity of the soil). The next day David went to the fields to sow the plaster, but to his surprise he found the work had been done. His sister, who lived near the field, said that her children had called her to watch three strangers the day before spread the plaster with remarkable skill. She assumed they were men David had hired."[1]

In the scriptures and in life, we read and hear of numerous times earthly messengers—like the three Nephites—are sent by a loving Father to help His children. Every one of us is impacted by earthly angels who come into our lives for a period of time and offer aid. Some are involved in our lives as family or friends for an extended time, while others may be involved but a moment and disappear, never to be seen again in this life. In some sacred cases, messengers leave an imprint upon our lives that is so lasting and so profound, it is never forgotten.

These lasting impressions may come through pure charity, crucial acts of service, a timely thought, comforting or healing words, a deep insight, a powerful testimony or an inspiring example. In these times, it is as if earthly angels are joining the three Nephites' desire and mission to "minister upon the face of the earth," thus becoming *a fourth Nephite.*

These servants of the Lord have not been physically transformed like the three Nephites, but in many ways they have been spiritually transformed through consecration and sacrifice to do and live the will of God. It was said of the three Nephites:

"And behold they will be among the Gentiles, and the Gentiles shall know them not.

They will also be among the Jews, and the Jews shall know them not" (3 Nephi 28:27-28). In many instances involving those I consider to be fourth Nephites, we, too, will never know their names or see them again in this life, but we will be impacted by their service and eternally blessed by their sacrifices.

I have felt the effects of a fourth Nephite time and time again as the Lord has extended a "multitude of his tender mercies" in my life (1 Nephi 8:8). I hope in some small way I, too, have been an instrument in the hands of God to deliver hope to a struggling soul as a fourth Nephite.

Elder Jeffrey R. Holland said, "But when we speak of those who are instruments in the hand of God, we are reminded that not all angels are from the other side of the veil. Some of them we walk with and talk with—here, now, every day. Some of them reside in our own neighborhoods. Some of them gave birth to us, and in my case, one of them consented to marry me"[2].

In my life, I have witnessed that an all-observing and an all-knowing God is constantly aware of His children every minute of every day.

I know there are times when He appropriately and thankfully sends someone from this earth to our aid. I have been the benefactor of this assistance on numerous occasions in my life at critical junctures and during desperate moments. I am so grateful that these earthly messengers of Heavenly Father are sent to minister to us in times of dire need.

Let me share a few examples of fourth Nephites in the right place at the right time who performed deeds that greatly impacted my life forever. A few years ago, my wife and I decided to take our young family on a trip to a resort town in Mexico.

Our kids were young and they were difficult to manage around the resort pools; we soon realized that four kids below eight-years old weren't ideal for this particular type of vacation. Because we had a small baby, an almost two-year old, a four-year old, and a seven-year old, we gravitated to the large toddler pool, which was about 18 inches deep, but fairly large. This was perfect for my sons Blake and Tanner who both couldn't really swim.

We had been swimming at these resort pools for two days, somewhat successfully. On the third morning at the pool, I went to get some lemonade for the family at the outdoor bar. While at the cashier, my son Tanner came running up to me and said, "Dad, Blake (*not quite 2-years-old*) almost drowned!" He told me Blake was across the baby pool from my wife when he tipped over and struggled to get his head out of the water. Mom, who was sitting with the baby in a baby carrier, ran across the pool in knee-deep water to rescue him. He was fine. Tanner took off to return to the pool. My wife then came over, with the rest of the family, and retold the near drowning experience. It was alarming, but I was grateful that all was well.

In a moment, my wife and I realized that four-year old Tanner had disappeared, so we quickly made our way toward the baby pool. As we approached the pool, I saw a lady fully clothed and soaking wet climbing out of the adult pool. She had our little boy right in front of her.

Apparently, when our son Tanner left me at the cashier, he ran back toward the pools, and, for some reason, he ran right for one of the adult pools, instead of the toddler pool, and dove in. There was no lifeguard and no guests at this pool, and Tanner couldn't swim on his own without flotation devices. Little Tanner was certainly going to drown that day.

At some point, this young lady in her early twenties— a fourth Nephite— was walking by the pool and happened to see Tanner sinking in the water. She watched for a moment and realized Tanner was not going to surface on his own. She quickly dove in—fully clothed with her wallet in her pocket and all—to save his young life.

When my wife and I walked up and saw this wet angel at the pool's edge, she explained what happened, and my heart swelled with gratitude for her and a loving God who had sent her at just the right time. I truly didn't know what to say or do other than thank her over and over again. I watched her as she fumbled for her wet wallet and attempted to walk back to her hotel room in soaked clothing. The episode was short and seemed to happen so fast. In the commotion, I never even asked her name. To this day I don't know who she was and I never saw her again. This heaven-sent lady changed my life and the life of my son. I know that I if I saw her today, I would not recognize her, but the impression she left on my life will last a lifetime. I will be forever grateful that she was sent to my son's aid and that she acted as a fourth Nephite that day.

During a critical time of my high school years, I encountered another remarkable fourth Nephite. This sweet teenager, full of charity and goodness, shared with me words of healing and encouragement that impacted my life when I desperately needed emotional and spiritual support. As a sophomore in high school, I was really struggling; my family and I were going through a lot. My father had recently left our family, and we were struggling emotionally, spiritually, and financially.

The burden on my mother was heavy as she was doing all in her power to make ends meet and raise five children. She was in school full-time, while also working a full-time job. We had moved to a new neighborhood, and I was at a high school where my old friends were going in different directions. I was struggling to make new friends and find my niche in life. I had always found solace in athletics, but I had stopped growing physically and was suddenly feeling very small emotionally. This resulted in the shrinking of my confidence and desire to participate in sports and other activities. I would say it was one of the hardest periods of my life, if not the hardest year of my life. It was difficult to go to my wonderful mother and tell her of my struggles because she, too, was barely surviving. Her burdens with the family felt heavy and desperate. During this low point and period of darkness in my life, there was one constant light that gave me some hope.

In my math class, I met a girl named Robin. Robin was a senior and, in my eyes, she was amazing. She was on the dance team at school, she was voted to the homecoming court, she was beautiful, happy, talented, popular, but most importantly, she was genuinely kind. She dated one of the big football players on campus, and so for me this was not about being in love with an older girl, it simply was about spiritual, emotional and social survival. I would look forward to seeing her everyday as she always had a smile, a hello, and usually a little bit of conversation for me. When I was in her presence, I felt like a dear friend, of great worth, handsome and wonderful.

At the end of the school year, Robin got a hold of my yearbook and wrote a beautiful note in it. I don't know if she wrote it because she noticed not many others had written or if she was sincere, but her note was life-changing. As a struggling fourteen-year old, I read Robin's note over and over again. This short and simple note from this heaven-sent earthly messenger came at a critical moment in my life. She spoke kind words of me, and she essentially told me that I was amazing. I didn't feel amazing, so her words lifted my spirits. She left me her phone number and said to call her during the summer.

I never did call her because I didn't need to after that. Robin's note and her kind words had done something incredible to my spirit and my heart; she helped instill in me a confidence, an assurance that I was of great worth. My confidence, which had been shaky at best, was beginning to return because of the actions and words of a fourth Nephite placed in my path right when I desperately needed help.

I am so grateful for Robin and what she did for me in writing two simple, yet life changing, paragraphs. Her words helped get me through a difficult period. Looking back, I am certain that Robin doesn't even remember writing that life-altering note to me that spring day. I am also certain that she had no idea that I clung to every word in her personal note. I also know that she had no idea that a loving God was using her as an instrument in a young, struggling boy's life.

Over the next year, things changed and I changed, and Heavenly Father blessed me in many ways as things got much better for me. Looking back, I am ever so grateful to a loving father for sending me a fourth Nephite to minister to me through kindness in a desperate time of need. After Robin graduated from high school, I never saw her again; she literally came into my life for one school year and then left, never to be seen again. Elder Holland reminds us, "Indeed heaven never seems closer than when we see the love of God manifested in the kindness and devotion of people so good and so pure that *angelic* is the only word that comes to mind"[3].

You may be asking yourself, *"Could I really be someone's fourth Nephite?"* The answer lies in defining what a fourth Nephite is. Fourth Nephites are unified in the purpose and hearts of the three Nephites in many ways. They desire to serve Christ forever above all else. They serve without hoping for something in return. They are inspired by the Spirit of God to call or visit when they are needed most. They are able to speak inspired words filled with the Spirit. They are able to testify of truth. They are able to lift, inspire, edify, and minister to those in need. They are, simply put, blessing the lives of others through Christ like desires and actions.

When I was nearing the completion of my degree at BYU, I was nervous that I was not yet married. A girl I was in love with had recently broken up with me so my dating life was not much to write home about. I didn't speak much of my concern to friends or others, but one day I bumped into a girl I had met a year earlier who had been a good friend to me. I hadn't seen her for some time, and we were able to catch up a little bit on each other's lives. For some reason on this occasion, she and I had a very deep conversation about love, marriage, and dating, and her words were just what I needed to hear. I still don't remember divulging my concerns with her, but I must have seemed concerned about my marital status.

She reminded me of the power of faith and righteousness. She told me that I was an amazing person, and that I lived my life in a way that I would be able to find someone wonderful. She was more impressed with me than I was impressed with myself. I don't know that her words were exactly true, but they gave me great confidence and inspired me to have faith and place my trust in God. Her words reminded me that there is power and promises in righteousness, and the Lord will bless the faithful. I left that conversation inspired and with a renewed desire to place my trust in the Lord.

After that conversation, I only saw her one or two more times in my life as she was married soon after our comforting conversation. Today, I simply recall a great and troubling weight lifted from me for a time because of some very powerful thoughts and words that blessed my life that day. Her words affected me in a manner that changed my hope, confidence and faith. I will be forever grateful for an hour with this sweet fourth Nephite.

Now that you know what to look for, you will see these fourth Nephites in so many instances. You and I have observed them as dedicated bishops who spend time counseling, Relief Society presidents who make inspired visits at just the right moment, powerful home teachers who know when to help a family in a time of need, and consistent visiting teachers whose love carries someone through a difficult time.

I have watched a true friend help another when they are leaning in the wrong direction. I have seen a priesthood holder offer and give priesthood blessings when they were desperately needed. I have witnessed youth leaders coming in to rescue a young man or woman in times of spiritual desperation. I have observed mothers, fathers, sisters and brothers play the role of fourth Nephites time and time again. Thank goodness for these consecrated individuals who have not been changed physically, but certainly have been spiritually made different because of the lives they live, their level of consecration, and the abundance of the Spirit they carry. I have learned that anyone who loves the Savior can be a fourth Nephite.

My stake president shared this story with me a few years ago. He said a sister had come into his office one day for comfort and counsel. She was discouraged and frustrated because she was living right, but she and her husband were struggling and unable to have the blessing of children in their life. She shared her feelings and sorrow with this good priesthood leader. He felt inspired to give her a priesthood blessing. In that heaven-sent blessing, she was promised she would have children.

The stake president resumed his busy life and hadn't thought much about the priesthood experience until she stopped by his home many months later. She dropped off her old, expired temple recommend to his wife while he was not home. When she handed the old recommend to the stake president's wife she said, "Please make sure and tell him that I am pregnant." Here was a sweet sister who wanted this good stake president to have a reminder of her and the comforting priesthood blessing he had given her. She will never forget that powerful priesthood blessing given to her by a fourth Nephite during a dire time of need.

When I think of fourth Nephite experiences, I see regular sons and daughters of God simply trying to serve Him and others the best way they know how. These earthly angelic individuals minister through love, service, inspiration, sacrifice, and testimony. They are able to change hearts and change lives through powerful impressions that they receive through the Spirit. Truly, fourth Nephites, like the three Nephites, "are as the angels of God" (3 Nephi 28:30).

Many years ago, my best friend's mother Bonnie passed away. She had been fighting cancer, but after a long battle, she eventually succumbed. Her kids were grown, she had been a wonderful mother, and there was a deep closeness in the family and a great love for this powerful woman. After her death and prior to the funeral, the children all congregated in Bonnie's home, but the mood was depressing. The children didn't really know what to say or what action they should take.

Into the dreary mood of this home at this difficult time walked Carol, a dear family friend. Carol didn't know what to do either, but she loved this family. Carol came in and went to work serving this family. She began talking, cleaning, moving, helping, and encouraging. Her efforts and her disposition lifted the spirits of the family. Soon the family all went to work. They began planning, talking, and attempting to lift one another. In a short time, the mood of the home changed, the spirits of the children changed, and great progress was made. Carol's angelic efforts truly elevated this family in a time of despair and sorrow. Within a short time and with elevated spirits, the family moved forward in faith and hope.

After the funeral, many of the family returned to their homes, but they never forgot Carol or her timely efforts. Whenever siblings in this family speak about their mother's funeral, Carol's name always comes up. For this family, a powerful memory of a mother's funeral is enhanced by Carol's ministering efforts in their desperate time of need. I know what a blessing Carol was to them as she is my mother and has blessed me thousands of times in my life.

I will never forget this fourth Nephite experience shared by Elder Vaughn J. Featherstone:

"A Relief Society president was at dinner. Suddenly she jumped up and said, "I've got to go!" Her husband asked, "Where are you going?" She answered, "I can't tell you. I'll be back later."

She was gone for about an hour. When she came back, her husband asked, "What was that all about?" She replied, "I had the strongest impression I had to go to the bishop's. I went over and knocked on the door. The bishop's wife came to the door, and I said, 'LaRae, I'm here. How can I help?'

The tears flowed down her cheeks, and she put her head down on my shoulder and wept. She said, 'You know, everybody loves my husband. He's the bishop. They bear testimony about him on Sunday and talk about what a great man he is. I'm not sure anybody in the ward even knows I'm here, knows I exist, or even cares. I wondered even if God cared or knew I was here. So I knelt down and prayed, "Heavenly Father, if you know I'm here or even care, please let me know.

And there was a knock on the door, and the Relief Society president said, "I'm here. How can I help?"4.

I have observed in life that not only are we the recipient of sacred fourth Nephite ministering experiences, but on occasion, the Lord allows us to be the fourth Nephite in these sacred experiences. Elder Holland shared this invitation: "In the process of praying for those angels to attend us, may we all try to be a little more angelic ourselves—with a kind word, a strong arm, a declaration of faith and "the covenant wherewith [we] have covenanted" (Jeffrey R. Holland October 2008 "The Ministry of Angels").

Just as we are all recipients of fourth Nephite experiences, we all need to strive to act as fourth Nephites. The Lord desperately needs instruments to perform sacred labors. The Lord needs consecrated individuals filled with the Spirit to heed His directives and perform His labors. As a bishop interviewing and visiting struggling members in the ward, I remember wanting so desperately to help so many people in a variety of ways. There was just no way humanly possible to satisfy so many needs. In every ward, in every congregation, in every area, the Lord is looking for fourth Nephites to be instruments in blessing His children to fulfill God's work and His mission.

I remember a deeply troubling and unforgettable visit with an active sister of my ward who appeared to have everything in the world going for her. She looked me in the eye and said, "There is not a person in this world who really cares about me. No one ever calls me or takes an interest in me." Those words penetrated my soul to the very core and caused a deep wound in my heart.

When I was the bishop of my ward, I was aware of numerous sisters who felt alone in their critical role of motherhood, but who continued to strive to patiently do the right thing. In many instances, I desperately desired one inspired sister to call, to recognize, to rescue, to acknowledge, to befriend, or to lift another in a time of desperate need. On some occasions I wondered to myself, "*Where are the sisters in Zion who could save this good sister?*"

In the instances where I observed a sister take action and faithfully respond to a need, I was always astonished and grateful. For me, these were moments of witnessing a true fourth Nephite come to the rescue of sisters yearning for attention, friendship, love and hope. President Spencer W. Kimball taught this concept when he said, "God does notice us, and he watches over us. But it is usually through another person that he meets our needs. Therefore, it is vital that we serve each other"[5].

I would like to share two examples from my life when I was blessed with opportunities to act as a fourth Nephite. I wish not to boast or highlight myself, but to testify what a privilege it is on occasion to be an instrument or a mouthpiece for a loving God to His children. As I share these thoughts, I am painfully aware of countless opportunities and numerous occasions when I could and should have been a mouthpiece or instrument in the Lord's hand and was not.

About five years ago, I went to a dental conference and met an old high school friend named Erin in the hallway. After returning from my full-time mission, I had spent a few weeks hanging out with Erin just before going to BYU. Erin was not a member of the church, so I had invited her to church and she attended a few times. I also tried to teach her the gospel of Jesus Christ. She seemed to enjoy the principles, but never fully embraced them. I went off to school and was busy again, and Erin and I lost contact with one another for twenty-five years, until five years ago at the dental conference.

At the conference, Erin told me how grateful she was to see me and that she had wanted to find me for many years to thank me for what I had done for her. I did not remember doing anything for her. She was now married, happy and pursuing some of her life's dreams. I was grateful to hear she was happy and doing well. She never converted to the gospel of Jesus Christ, but she did share some kind thoughts.

She said, "For years I have wanted to talk to you and thank you." Bewildered, I asked, "Why?" She said words to this effect, "When we were friends after your mission, I was at a point in my life when I was struggling deeply with some things and trying to figure out who I was, what I wanted to be, and what direction I wanted to go in. You came into my life for a moment and were a great example of living your religion and being content and different. Your example caused me to give up some bad habits and increased my desire to be more committed to Christ and strengthened my faith."

She stated that she had remained much more committed to Christ and to righteous values in her life. She then thanked me, and I have not seen her since that tender ten-minute meeting five years ago.

I was flattered by her words, but there was an immediate realization on my part that it had not been me, but a loving God who knew Erin could do better and be more committed to good. At that crucial point in her life, I was used as a temporary instrument in the hands of God. I am grateful to know God could use me as an instrument to bless her at a critical time. I was grateful to see Erin that day and thankful for her words, but I was most grateful for my Heavenly Father reminding me that I need to constantly be a minister and disciple of truth.

The second example falls under the umbrella of my days as a bishop. One day a good woman named Kim (who was not a member of the church) was having some serious marital struggles. She had many trials at the time, and a good friend of hers wanted her to have a priesthood blessing. We knew Kim, as she had been a friend of the family for a few years. The arrangements were made for me to give Kim a priesthood blessing. I remember feeling Kim was prepared for the gospel and pleading desperately that she would feel something from the blessing. The Lord answered my prayer that day as Kim had a powerful experience during the blessing. She felt the Spirit of God and the hand of God touch her life. What a privilege it was to be a voice for Heavenly Father and be a small instrument in Kim's life.

This sacred priesthood blessing moved Kim as it strengthened her in a significant time of need. A few weeks following the priesthood blessing, Kim began taking the missionary discussions. Through the discussion process, Kim received another witness of the truthfulness of the gospel of Jesus Christ. It was just a few weeks after the priesthood blessing that Kim was baptized into the church. I remember feeling so blessed as I watched Heavenly Father work His miracle in the life of this sweet, prepared sister Kim.

Full-time missionaries in many instances are like fourth Nephites to so many of the people they meet, teach, and serve. Missionaries come into so many precious lives bearing a sacred message that is life-changing, and then—

after a short time—they depart for a new area, or new assignment, or even for home. In many instances, they will never see these beloved people again until they walk through celestial doors. These wonderful people who receive the riches of eternity from missionaries bearing truth, light, peace, hope, and life's answers, will forever be touched by emissaries playing the role of fourth Nephites.

Not too long ago, a new couple, the Danielsons, moved into my previous ward. The Danielsons were fun, energetic, and had burning testimonies of the gospel of Jesus Christ. Brother Danielson had just been released as a stake president and his good wife was a ball of fire. They each spoke in the ward, served where they could, and then they left to a new area where they had been building a home five months later. On their final Sunday in our ward before moving into their new home, Brother Danielson bore a powerful testimony of Christ when he echoed Joseph and Sidney Rigdon's words. He stated his testimony was plain and simple like the two brothers' testimony when they said, "And now after the many testimonies which have been given of him, this is the testimony, last of all, which we give of him: That he lives" (D&C 76:22). Nephi said, "after ye had received the Holy Ghost ye could speak with the tongue of angels...Angels speak by the power of the Holy Ghost; wherefore, they speak the words of Christ" (2 Nephi 32:2-3). These powerful words on this occasion were angelic.

He emphasized those priceless two words: "He lives." His testimony had a weighty effect upon me because it was Spirit-filled, unforgettable and simply profound. I have reflected on those precious, life-altering two words, "He lives." Those angelic words have changed the course of my life for good. I was grateful for a powerful reminder through the testimony of a man that I may never see again. This good brother came subtly in my life, and, despite not knowing him very well, he had a profound impact upon me through the power of a simple statement and moving testimony.

In life, you will encounter people who will only remember one act of your service, one thought you shared, one testimony you bore or one impression you left. May you be like a fourth Nephite to those you encounter; serve them, love them, inspire them, and testify to them of truths which are life changing. Like the three Nephites, may it be said of you: "great and marvelous works shall be wrought by them" (3 Nephi 28:31).

Recently, I was sitting on the beach with my family and extended family and was speaking with my mom. She is nearly 80 years old and has lived a tremendous life. She has been a principal of thousands of middle and high school students. She has been a licensed nurse to thousands more. She has held numerous other jobs. She has been a mother of six, and a grandmother to more than thirty. She has been a friend and an advocate to many. She has served in numerous capacities in the church with a long stint as Relief Society President, among other callings.

I asked her a question that caused her serious reflection, "Mom, in your lifetime, what is the greatest thing you feel you have done?" I really didn't know what her response would be or what I was even looking for. I loved that she really contemplated the question. Then she surprised me with her response by saying, "I think the greatest thing I have done in my life is my service to others."

I believe her response is comparable to the sentiments shared by the three Nephites when the Savior said of them, "for ye have desired that ye might bring the souls of men unto me, while the world shall stand" (3 Nephi 28:9). Bless those fourth Nephites like my mother, who serve their entire lives, in an attempt to bring souls closer to Christ through Christ like service.

Remember this promise from a modern apostle: "And always there are those angels who come and go all around us, seen and unseen, known and unknown, mortal and immortal"[6]. May we constantly express gratitude to God for the earthly angels or fourth Nephites who profoundly impact our lives. May we also strive to fulfill the role of a fourth Nephite by being sensitive to the Spirit so that we may profoundly bless the lives of others.

Notes

1.   "Coming Forth of the Book of Mormon and the Restoration of the Priesthood," Church History in the Fullness of Times Student Manual (Salt Lake City: The Church of Jesus Christ of Latter Day Saints, 2003), 56-57.

2.   Jeffrey R. Holland, "The Ministry of Angels," Ensign, November 2008.

3.   Ibid.

4.   Vaughn J. Featherstone, "Things Too Wonderful for Me," BYU Devotional, Feb 13, 2001.

5.   Spencer W. Kimball, Teachings of Presidents of the Church: Spencer W.

Kimball (Salt Lake City: The Church of Jesus Christ of Latter Day Saints, 2006), 82.

6.   Ibid.

About the Author

As a young man, Jeff served a full-time mission in the Canada Halifax Mission. Jeff and his amazing wife, Christine, have six sons and one daughter and reside in Gilbert, Arizona.

Jeffrey "Jeff" Erickson has been a youth speaker at Especially For Youth (EFY) for many years. He has served faithfully in many capacities in the church including gospel doctrine instructor and bishop. He has a passion for writing and speaking about the gospel of Jesus Christ.

Jeff is one of the co-founders of NSFC (Non-Sunday futbol club) Strikers. This soccer club is the first non-Sunday competitive soccer club in Arizona. He is the recent author of "A Weekly Letter to Your Missionary". He has published a youth-related story in the New Era called "Catch". His website is www.missionaryletter.com.

Made in the USA
San Bernardino, CA
24 December 2018